God's Way to Prosper
"I Used to Be Broke"

By

Raymond Delone

Table of Contents

Acknowledgments 4

Forward 5

Introduction 7

Tithe and Offering 11

Protecting Your Household 23

The Emergency Fund 32

The Retirement Account 36

Protecting Your Assets 40

Managing Your Debts 44

The Balance Sheet 50

The Income Profile 54

Creating Wealth 56

Wealth Distribution 59

Summary 61

One Last Action 63

Scripture References 64

Appendix New Spending Habits Worksheet 73

Action Plan Forms 78

Acknowledgments

To all of my clients. I am grateful for all of the years you allowed me to serve you. May God continue to bless you. This book is a tribute to you and the hours and years you allowed me to discuss finances during appointments. My life has been enriched because of you.

Thank you to Mary Hendricks, Anna Christian, and Sterling Delone for your help and encouragement. Special thanks to Jacquay Durant and Dr. Annette Thomas for putting the finishing touches on this book.

Forward

Thank you! I really appreciate it. This has truly been a blessing...a complete eye-opener that is life-changing. *Brigitte Watkins*

Thank you for helping me with my finances... I really appreciate your advice. *Edwina Harry*

Thank you and I pray that God bless you a prophet's reward for teaching us to be better stewards. *Toi Johnson*

I thank you for what I have received, it has jump-started me on my path to financial recovery. *Tina Williams*

Thanks for being an awesome teacher. *Lisa Flot*

Thank you so much for aiding me in my financial services. Prayer and blessings. *Lorene Robinson*

I wanted to tell you that when I met with you two years ago, I was over-extended with credit cards a personal loan and a car loan. Since I saw you, I have paid off most of my credit cards using a consolidation. Even though consolidation is not the perfect solution I can concentrate on a single payment each month. Now I only have my car payment and the loan. I am retired now so this makes it easier to pay my bills. I was probably paying more than eighty percent a year in interest including my car note. Thanks so much for your sound advice. God Bless. *Carolyn Smith*

I read your book. Lots of good information. I could relate to a lot of it, particularly the part about getting started on the path. I'm well on my way. Good Luck! *Sterling Delone*

Introduction

I have been in the financial service business for over thirty-five years. I have prepared thousands of income tax returns, represented hundreds of buyers and sellers in real estate transactions, and have written many annuities and life insurance policies. In my thirty-five years, very few of my clients have implemented the strategies of the wealthy. Most of my clients, including my Christian clients, have not put into practice the art of creating, managing, and distributing wealth.

Allow me to share with you two major principles I have discovered about finances and financial transactions. First, the world has a system of attaining income, wealth, and riches. For example, have you heard these statements? Go to school… get a good education… get a good job…retire with the company's gold watch. How about: make all you can…can all you get… and sit on the can!

The world's system of attaining income, wealth and riches usually depends on who you know, what school you graduated from, and what you are willing to compromise along the way. This world's system affords you the opportunity to work thirty to forty years to earn money while simultaneously and meticulously devising advertisements that lure your money away from you as quickly as you earn it. The world's system spends billions of dollars on advertising annually to entice you into spending your thirty to forty years of wealth on cars, houses, and consumable goods. The end result is most people retire in debt, and live on social security; some retirees fair a little better and retire with social security and a small pension.

Did you know the average American retirement income is barely over $1,500 per month, $18,000 annually, according to the Pension Rights Center? Facts show that most households do not live on a budget; they consume their income, wealth and riches without any consideration on how to allocate it to the immediate or future needs of their household.

There is a saying in the business world, if you ran a business like you ran your family budget, you would be in jail for embezzlement.

Most families, including Christians, do not have a plan of action when it comes to creating, managing, and distributing their wealth, so by nature of default the money that should have been used for one thing is misused for another. This is called "impulse spending," or as I heard recently, "therapeutic spending." Unfortunately, most Americans are professionals at spending their future income, wealth and riches prematurely.

In the world's system, income, wealth and riches are usually obtained by working, buying stocks, bonds, investing in real estate, starting or purchasing an existing business, franchise, or inventing something the world feels it cannot do without.

The second principle I discovered is God has a system for attaining income, wealth and riches. Proverbs 10:22 says, *"The blessing of the Lord, brings wealth, without painful toil for it."* Deuteronomy 8:18 says, *"But remember the Lord your God, for it is He who gives you the ability to produce wealth."* God wants you blessed, spiritually, physically and materially.

God's system of attaining income, wealth and riches is a superior system that allows you to prosper without limits, and within a framework of honesty and integrity. Proverbs 14:12 says, *"There is a way that appears to be right, but in the end, it leads to death."* Matthew 16:26 says, *"What good will it be for a man if he gains the whole world, yet forfeits his soul? Or what can a man give in exchange for his soul?"* For the believer, the methods mentioned above for gaining income, wealth and riches are not bad strategies if they are inspired and directed by the leading of the Holy Spirit.

Most people, including Christians, do not connect God with their finances, they fail to understand the relationship between the two. There are many scriptures in the Bible that connect your financial wellbeing to the word of God. My prayer is that this book will help you practically apply the scriptures and put you in a position for God's word to fulfill its purpose in your life!

Raymond Delone

Chapter 1

Tithe and Offering

We must ask ourselves: why should we be concerned with how we handle our money? The Apostle Paul writes, *"For we brought nothing into this world, and it is certain we can carry nothing out"* (1 Timothy 6:7).

So how important is our income and our ability to create wealth and riches? Wealth, and the ability to get it is a part of God's plan for our lives.

Even though we cannot take our income, wealth and riches with us after death, we must be good stewards with what God has entrusted to us here on Earth. Matthew 25:21 says, *His master replied, "Well done, good and faithful servant! You have been faithful with a few things; I will put you in charge of many things..."* and Luke 16:10-12 says, *"Whoever can be trusted with very little can also be trusted with much, and whoever is dishonest with very little will also be dishonest with much. So, if you have not been trustworthy in handling worldly wealth, who will trust you with true riches? And if you have not been trustworthy with someone else's property, who will give you property of your own?"*

In Matthew 25:15-21 it was the ones who multiplied their resources, wealth who received the praise. We will all have to give an account of our financial stewardship one day.

How does good stewardship affect our money and lifestyle? We all know money or the lack of it affects every decision we make in life. We all make our buying decisions whether in restaurants, purchasing a home or giving in church based on our resources (money). The amount of money we have readily available determines our actions and our generosity with others and the kingdom of God ministries.

I begin to ponder, if God, is my source as stated in Philippians 4:19, why do I and so many Christians have so many needs? If I shall not want as stated in Psalm 23:1, why am I and so many other Christians in want? And lastly, if I will delight myself in the Lord, He will give me the desires of my heart as stated in Psalm 37:4, why do I and other Christians still have unfulfilled desires?

I believe the book of Haggai 1:5-7 gives us a clue: *Now this is what the Lord Almighty says: "Give careful thought to your ways. You have planted much but have harvested little. You eat, but never have enough. You drink, but never have your fill. You put on clothes but are not warm. You earn wages, only to put them in a purse with holes in it." This is what the Lord Almighty says: "Give careful thought to your ways."*

The book of Numbers 23:19 adds more clarity on where the disconnect with God is, *"God is not a man, that he should lie, nor a son of man, that he should change his mind. Does he speak and then not act? Does he promise and not fulfill?"*

After considerable time and thought, God gave me this *Action Plan* to share with clients to assist them in organizing their financial priorities.

The *Action Plan* redirects resources to create, manage and distribute wealth, God's way. Each part of the *Action Plan* is designed to place you in a position to increase, maintain or safeguard your wealth. As you read the following chapters you will be given the *Action Plan* component and the order of their priority. Each chapter is written with one or more components in mind. See forms in the back of the book for the complete *Action Plan - Establishing New Spending Habits, Balance Sheet* and *Income Profile.*

We will go line by line and emphasize the importance of each component. As we move down the *Action Plan* W*orksheets*, you will have suggested dollar amounts for each component. The *Action Plan* is most effective if prepared annually and most importantly put into action!

The *Spiritual Application*: **Bring the whole tithe into the storehouse, that there may be food in my house. Test me in this, "says the Lord Almighty, and see if I will not throw open the floodgates of heaven and pour out so much blessing that you will not have room enough to store it"** (Malachi 3:1). **"Honor the Lord by** *giving him the first part of all your income, and he will fill your barns with wheat and barley and overflow your wine vats with the finest wines"* (Proverbs 3:9).

These scriptures clearly connect the tithe and offering to God's system of attaining income, wealth and riches. There is a spiritual blessing attached to our obedience when acting on the word of God.

Remember God's system for attaining income, wealth and riches is different and far superior to the world's system. Why is God's system better? It allows you to prosper without limits, and within a framework of honesty and integrity. It's not based on who you know, what school you graduated from, or what you are willing to compromise along the way.

As you see from the above scriptures the tithe and offering are vital to our financial well-being. It is our number one priority and the first step on our *Action Plan*.

In my thirty-five years of being in the financial service business, I have noticed two glaring facts: people who do not give tithes and offerings often have money problems. They somehow never seem to have enough money to meet their financial obligations. They have one hundred percent of their take-home pay and yet cannot make ends meet.

Many are unaware that giving the tithe and offering will create cash-flow possibilities. Two books of the Old Testament reinforce this concept, Hosea 4:6 says, "*My people are destroyed from a lack of knowledge*:" and the book of Malachi 3:11 says, *"He will rebuke the devourer for your sake."* If you need more clarity 2 Corinthians 9:8 says, **"God is able to make all grace abound to you, so that in all things at all times, having all that you need, you will abound in every good work."**

The second glaring fact is even after giving your tithe and offering if you are not disciplined: with the remaining eighty-plus percent, you will not become wealthy, instead you will experience the opposite which is poverty. I know this may sound like a contradiction to the above scriptures, it's not! In our current society, most people do not set aside a part of their wealth to create more wealth. We will talk more about this later.

The book of James 2:26 says, ... *"For as the body without the spirit is dead, so faith without works is dead also."* We must put legs to our faith, it is not enough to just hope or believe our finances will change without having corresponding actions.

Unfortunately, in most churches, this is exactly what you hear, if you give your tithes and offerings your financial needs will be met. This is only a partial truth, you must be a good steward of the hundred percent of your income, not just the tithe and offering portion. This is where the problem lies, we will talk more about this in the coming chapters. Each time you receive your paycheck, commission or whatever legitimate income source you receive, take a portion of that income and place it into your giving account.

You must be faithful to tithe and give an offering on all income no matter how large or small. The tithe is ten percent of your income and the offering is any amount above your tithe you desire. Remember your harvest depends on your giving (2 Corinthians 9:6-8). The tithe is your first step in your journey trusting God's word for an increase. It may help to remember you are only giving ten cents of every dollar as a tithe and however the Lord leads you in giving an offering. Remember: your ten percent may be large or small. However, the blessing is in your obedience, not the amount. As we go further, we will talk about the remaining eighty-plus percent of income.

Keep in mind we are using God's system for attaining income, wealth and riches. The tendency for most people is if your income is large, you will not tithe because you feel it is too much money to give away, and on the other side of that coin if your income is small, you will not tithe because you are embarrassed the amount is too little. Either choice disconnects you from God's system of gaining income, wealth and riches.

The *Practical Application*: In the world's system, the tithe and offering also have a benefit. They are tax-deductible on our income tax return, if we itemized our deductions, the tithe and offerings can help lower our income tax liability. Paying less income taxes means more wealth for you.

The median household income in the United States is $56,516 according to 2015 data from the U.S. Census. As an example, using the median household income and our *Income Profile Worksheet*, your net monthly income is $3523.86 (see *Chapter 8 Income Profile*). The tithe is ten percent $352.39, and let's say you chose to give $88.10, 2.5% of your income as an offering.

This is an example your household income may be more or less. On your *Establishing New Spending Habits Worksheet,* you will enter:
Tithe: $352.39
Offering: $88.10
Total: $440.49

Place this amount in your giving account as soon as you receive it. It does not matter if you receive your income daily, weekly, monthly or bi-monthly. Your tithe is ten percent, and your offering is any amount you decide in addition to your tithe. Now you have positioned yourself to be a happy hilarious giver!

Why do we need a written *Action Plan*? *"And the Lord answered me, and said, Write the vision, and make it plain upon tables, that he may run that readeth it. For the vision is yet for an appointed time, but at the end it shall speak, and not lie: though it may tarry, wait for it; because it will surely come…"* (Habakkuk 2:2-3).

A written vision or plan gives you clarity of purpose and reinforces your stated desire. The plan is not yet manifested, but with determination and action, it will appear. Your *Action Plan* highlights your financial vision. Every household *Action Plan* is different.

To manage your finances, you need to open multiple bank accounts. Don't panic, you can have multiple accounts at more than one bank. Each category on your *Action Plan* has to have a separate bank account. If you put all of your money into the same account you will misallocate it. Remember the saying "don't put all your eggs into one basket!" This may sound extreme, but in reality, it's not! You want an account that has no minimum balance or monthly service fee. If this is not possible choose the financial institution with the lowest minimum balance and fees.

The *Action Plan* works most effectively when you get the money out of your hands immediately and into its designated account.

Even though your earning power (income) increases over your years of employment because most household's including Christians do not live on a budget, the chances to misallocate and continue impulse spending are dramatically increased.

It's been said, "it takes twenty-one days to develop a new habit." Be patient with yourself and be determined to fully implement your *Action Plan*.

Chapter 2

Protecting Your Household

Most household budgets will include, shelter, your rent or mortgage, groceries and eating out, utilities: electric, heating, water, cable, landline, internet, DSL, household goods, and transportation.

The Spiritual Application: ***"But if any provide not for his own, and specially, for those of his own house, he hath denied the faith, and is worse than an infidel"*** (1Timothy 5:8).

The Practical Application: I don't know your personal story, but here is a glimpse of mine about twenty-four years ago. In 1989 I relocated from my first home, 800 square feet, two-bedroom one bath. Mortgage payments $283 included principle, interest, taxes, and insurance. I purchased a brand new 1800 square feet, four bedrooms two and one-half bath home. Mortgage payments $1175, principle and interest.

I was in my early thirty's, married with three children, things were going well for about four years. My income source was from selling real estate and preparing income taxes. Before the move, I could close one escrow and pay about six to twelve months of mortgage payments, depending on the sales price. Can you see where I'm going? Add to the situation I am now commuting seventy miles one-way, three to four days a week, and about five to six days a week during income tax season.

I went from using a TV antenna on the roof to paying a cable bill each month. Eighty percent of my income was generated from real estate sales. In 1990 the real estate market crashed, it took about three years before my bills exceeded my income and reserves. Real estate sales commission was my only income except during tax season. My point is, I had to make some major decisions. What bills to pay? How do I buy time with my creditors? How do I maintain my mortgage?

I was a tither before the real estate market crashed, and I was determined to continue tithing. I was not paying myself; that revelation came much later. It took about two years to pay all of my creditors and get back on track. I was determined not to file bankruptcy because I knew, it was not my spending habits, it was a lack of income. Just a side note: it's been my observation most people who file bankruptcy never change their spending habits and end up, back in debt. I did have an offer of compromise on one debt and debt forgiveness on another.

I stayed faithful in giving my tithes first, then paying my home mortgage and juggling everything else. My confession of faith was if I had to use an ice chest for my refrigerator and candles for lights, I was determined to keep my home and pay my tithes. I did not know at the time this was a confession of faith but looking back that is exactly what it was. I never missed giving a tithe nor a mortgage payment. To God be the glory!

Thank God I only had my mortgage, a few credit cards, utilities: phone, electric, gas, water, cable and of course food and gasoline. This was still a big deal my income was commission only. I was forced to call my utility companies and make payment arrangements every month, pretty much robbing Peter to pay Paul. I called my creditors and told them I could only pay them in essence after paying my top priorities... tithes, housing, food, transportation and utilities. I found myself telling some creditors you are third, fourth or fifth on my list depending on available income for that month. It took about two years but everyone received their money. Of course, my credit suffered, but today I have great credit and very little debt.

You may be in a similar situation, over-encumbered, more bills than income, robbing Peter to pay Paul. Using the *Establishing New Spending Habits Worksheet,* allowed me to re-direct my spending, and to trust God for wisdom and grace. Genesis 18:14 says, ***"Is anything too hard for the Lord?"*** I am not advocating irresponsibility! The Bible says, ***Evil men borrow and "cannot pay it back!" But the good man returns what he owes with some extra besides*** (Psalm 37:21).

I know this may sound extreme, give your tithes and offering, opening multiple bank accounts, paying yourself first. Remember most people work thirty to forty years and earn hundreds of thousands of dollars and retire in poverty. If you are already behind what do you have to lose? If you are not behind, good stewardship will increase your resources and wealth. If you choose not to allocate your income, wealth and riches in this order, you will probably never develop the financial discipline to create the power to get wealth. When you are over-encumbered and you continue to pay bills first, three things happen: your tithes and offerings never get to the storehouse, as mentioned in Malachi 3:10, you never accumulate savings and you continue to struggle. It's a vicious cycle!

But if you choose to tithe, give an offering and pay yourself first, you have just empowered yourself. Remember the Bible says the wicked don't repay their debt. We must be faithful in our re-payment of debt. We will talk more about the process of debt repayment later.

Back to our *Establishing New Spending Habits Worksheet*. As an example, let's say your shelter; rent or mortgage is $1785 per month, groceries $660, electric $175, water $100, heating $50, cable $106, cell phone $50 and transportation $320. Your amounts may be larger or smaller. On your *Establishing New Spending Habits Worksheet*, you will enter:

Shelter:	$1785
Groceries:	$660
Utilities:	$481
Transportation:	$320

Total: $3,246

You must open a bank account for each category. Even though your household budget may have many more categories, your top four priorities must be shelter, food, utilities, and transportation. These are your basic needs, everything else could be considered a luxury! Remember: I mentioned earlier if God is my source, as stated in Philippians 4:19 why do I and so many Christians have so many needs?

Consumerism is such a huge part of our American lifestyle; we are blindsided by commercialism. We do not see the big picture, we fall prey to spending our income, wealth and riches on consumption. I am not of the religion of no holidays. I marvel at major merchants, and I know industry is the bloodline of the world's system. You probably have your favorite retailer, but for this example, I will use Walmart. I have nothing personally against the company, I often shop there. However, I do marvel at their selling techniques, ten of the twelve months of the year they launch huge sale promotions. They use professional signage and banners, to lure consumers to their aisles of merchandise for consumption. They are the world's number one retailer. They have mastered the art of selling merchandise so well, we just follow their signs and spend our income, wealth and riches. To illustrate how deep-seated this-urge to spend is, if we do not purchase when the shelves are full (in a timely manner) we often settle for what is left (or walk away feeling guilty) for not purchasing something!

We are systematically driven to purchase promotional goods in addition to our everyday needs. The spending push begins in February with Valentine's Day. April, Easter. May, Mother's Day and Memorial Day. June, Father's Day and Graduation Day. July, the 4th of July. August, Back to School. September, Labor Day. October, Halloween. November, Veterans Day, Thanksgiving and the newest spending trend,

Black Friday, ending the year with Christmas. Just a side note: add Income Tax Season, January through April 15, most consumers have additional income. As mentioned earlier without an *Action Plan*, we foolishly give our income, wealth and riches away.

Remember most households, including Christians, do not live on a budget. Your rent or mortgage payment is the only fixed amount, the other categories will increase or decrease. A written budget will help you recognize which category needs the most attention. When it comes to protecting your household, allocate your money, wealth on these top four priorities first. Any remaining money will flow into the other categories on your *Establishing New Spending Habits Worksheet*.

Include all monthly expenses on the *New Spending Habits Worksheet*, even if expenses exceed your monthly income. Listing all of your expenses will help you determine which expenses are necessary and within your income budget. The goal is to spend your resources on the most important category first. I believe if you use your income, wealth and riches in this way you will see that God does supply your need. Matthew 6:33 says, *"But seek first his kingdom and his righteousness, and all these things will be given to you as well."*

If you have exhausted your monthly income, on the first two components, it's okay. Call your creditors and explain your hardship, let them know you have rearranged your budget and you are working through your shortage. Of course, your credit may suffer; however, you are redirecting your income, wealth and riches to work for you.

If you are over-encumbered, more bills than income, robbing Peter to pay Paul, establish new spending habits, give your tithe and offering first, then protect your household. Be patient with yourself and persistent with your new spending and saving habits: this will require a determined mindset and a change of behavior: Trust God for increase!

Chapter 3

The Emergency Fund

The Spiritual Application: Knowing and acting on the Word of God activates an ever-present emergency fund. The book of Hosea 4:6 says, *"My people are destroyed from a lack of knowledge."* God promises if you tithe and give offerings, *"He will rebuke the devourer for your sake"* Malachi 3:11. The Bible also declares **"God is able to make all grace abound to you, so that in all things at all times, having all that you need, you will abound in every good work"** (2 Corinthians 9:8). These scriptures put you in a position to receive the blessing, that will generate surplus and overflow; however, remember you must be a good steward of the hundred percent of the "blessing," (income), you received, not just the tithe and offering portion.

The Practical Application: The emergency fund is your "got you fund." The car breaks down, the water heater goes out, you have to travel out of town unexpectedly. Your emergency fund account keeps you from using credit cards or borrowing money in times of an unexpected cash event.

A fully-funded emergency account is three to six months of expenses. Use the *Establishing New Spending Habits Worksheet* to total your current monthly spending. Take your total monthly expense and multiply it by six. This amount is your target goal for this account. This may be a stretch for most people, start where you are! Depending on where you are financially, you may have to start your account with $50.00. Deposit something into your emergency fund account each time you receive your paycheck, commission or retirement income.

If all of your monthly resources are already allocated take one dollar from one of the categories in Chapter 2, deposit it into your emergency fund. At this stage, it is not the amount it is the discipline we want to develop. We will talk more about this in (Chapter 6, *Managing Your Debts)*. Since you need a separate account for each category and you cannot open a bank account with a dollar, I suggest putting the money in a jar until you have the minimum amount to open an account. Be patient with yourself this is a process.

Once your account is opened allocate something into your account each time you receive income, wealth and riches. This account then will take on a life of its own as you diligently work your plan and trust God. Proverbs 13:11 says, *"Dishonest money dwindles away, but he who gathers money little by little makes it grow."*

Continue to implement your *Action Plan*. The goal is to fully fund this account as soon as possible. As God increases your income, wealth and riches increase the amount going into your emergency fund.

"No discipline seems pleasant at the time, but painful. Later on, however, it produces a harvest of righteousness and peace for those who have been trained by it" (Hebrew 12:11).

Back to our *Establishing New Spending Habits Worksheet*. As an example, let's say your total annual expenses are $32,652. To fully fund your emergency account, you need three to six months of income. To arrive at your monthly amount, divide $32,652 by two, then divide that amount by twelve. On your *Establishing New Spending Habits Worksheet*, you will enter: Emergency Fund: $1,360.50

Your expenses and emergency fund may be more or less. If you cannot fully fund your Emergency Fund in twelve months, deposit as much as you can in the first year. Continue making deposits until you reach your maximum goal. When an emergency happens, use your emergency fund account, not credit cards or payday loans. Remember to replenish your account, God has given you the power to get wealth. Your emergency fund account is a part of that wealth.

Just a side note: most people never seriously consider their financial plight. Keep in mind we are using God's system for attaining income, wealth and riches. By trusting God and implementing your *Action Plan*, you are positioning yourself to achieve your goals based on biblical principles. Do not base God's ability to bless you based on your financial limitations.

Here's a good scripture to meditate on: ***"Now faith is the substance of things hoped for, the evidence of things not seen"*** (Hebrews 11:1).

35

Chapter 4

The Retirement Account

The Spiritual Application: ***For the Lord your God is bringing you into a good land; a land with streams and pools of water, with springs flowing in the valleys and hills; a land with wheat and barley, vine and fig trees, pomegranates, olive oil and honey; a land where bread will not be scarce and you will lack nothing...*** *(*Deuteronomy 8:7-9).

"For I know the plans I have for you, declares the Lord, plans to prosper you and not to harm you, plans to give you hope and a future" (Jeremiah 29:11). Remember: earlier I mentioned the world's system and their concept of retirement... "Go to school, get a good education, get a good job..." "Make all you can; can all you get, and sit on the can!" The above scriptures far surpass the world's system. The world's view of wealth is millions of dollars. However, most people were not born as the saying goes "with a silver spoon in their mouth."

I want to retire in a place as nice and pleasant as the one in (Deuteronomy 8:7-11). So how do we get to a place like this in the natural?

The Practical Application: There are many ways to start saving for your retirement. Fully fund your pension plan at work especially if your employer matches your contribution. Open an IRA account if your employer does not offer a retirement plan. An individual retirement arrangement (IRA) is an account set up at a financial institution that allows an individual to save for retirement with tax-free growth or on a tax-deferred basis. Invest in a primary home if you are not a homeowner. Purchase residential rental real estate for passive income and equity appreciation. Open a TD Ameritrade account and invest in the stock market or mutual funds. Start your retirement account as soon as you can. Building wealth is a process.

God will give you many opportunities to attain income, wealth and riches in your lifetime. Be sensitive to His leading and obey His commands. Following God's lead will open many doors and avenues to godly success. Listen to the Holy Spirit, this is when you will have your greatest opportunity to obtain income, wealth and riches.

I once heard this statement, if I could only get back the stupid money I spent, I would be wealthy. Does that resonate with you?

After reading *The Richest Man in Babylon* I learned how to accelerate the wealth process. One statement in the book changed my mindset, it said, a part of all I earn, is mines to keep. That was the missing link! I had faithfully given my tithe and offering, paid my mortgage, expenses, and debt. I was blessed with a home, two rental properties and a commercial building, however, I was cash poor. After reading that one statement it challenged me to take another step of faith. Save a part of all I earn. Following this principle is a sure way to increase your wealth and riches.

The concepts and strategies I'm sharing were acquired in my thirty-five years working in the financial service business. They say hindsight is twenty-twenty. My suggestion is if you are under thirty years old, save 10% of your income each year. If you are over thirty, save 15 to 20% of your income each year. This money can fund your emergency account first, then your company retirement plan or your IRA retirement account up to the deductible amount.

As an example, using the median household income and the *Income Profile Worksheet* (see example in Chapter 8). On your *Establishing New Spending Habits Worksheet*, you will enter: Retirement: $704.77

Your *New Spending Habits Worksheet* is a blueprint of who you are now and by re-directing your income, wealth and riches presents who you can become. Here is a scripture to stand on: ***"He will bless them that fear the Lord, both small and great. The Lord shall increase you more and more, you and your children"*** (Psalm 115:13-14).

Chapter 5

Protecting Your Assets

Insurance products play a vital role in protecting your assets, yet insurance products can be viewed as a waste of money, a necessary evil if you pay your premiums and never file a claim. However, if you have an unexpected death, auto accident, or health issue, the premiums paid become a prudent investment, a blessing in disguise. No matter how you feel about insurance (e.g., Life, Homeowners, Auto, Health, Dental and Renter's) all are key components in your financial budget.

The Spiritual Application: *"Wisdom is the principal thing; therefore, get wisdom: and with all thy getting get understanding"* (Proverbs 4:7).

Our spiritual application is worth repeating, wisdom is the principal thing. Good stewardship includes protecting your assets; your life, health, home, and belongings. Adequate insurance coverage is a must! Unfortunately, many people choose not to have insurance on their most important asset.

According to Bestliferate.org, 2017 Life Insurance Statistics and Facts, reports 41% of Americans do not carry any life insurance. Of those who do, nearly a third have just a basic group policy.

Life insurance products come with many names: Whole Life, Term, Variable Life, Adjustable Life, Universal Life, Index Universal, Burial, Return of Premiums and Mortgage insurance, just to name a few. However, life insurance can be categorized as either Whole Life or Term insurance, all other life products are a variation of the two.

Of the two basic products, I believe Term Insurance is the best value dollar for dollar. For example, a thirty-year-old male, non-smoker, in good health can purchase a $500,000 thirty-year Term Insurance policy for about $36 a month versus, a Whole Life policy for about $376 a month. In the event of death life insurance can be a replacement of income or just a way to create an immediate estate for your loved ones. Life insurance death benefit proceeds are tax-free.

If you are a homeowner, adequate homeowner's insurance is another important component of your wealth-building process. Review your section 1 coverage: Dwelling, Other Structures, Personal Property, Loss of Use, Personal Liability, and Guest Medical Payments annually. Liability coverage is very inexpensive, make sure you have enough, no less than, $1,000,000. Being underinsured or paying too much for inadequate coverage can be discovered during this process. Stay abreast of home values in your area make sure your dwelling coverage is correct. If you rent, get renter's insurance it is very inexpensive.

Auto Insurance can be expensive, to help lower your cost always bundle your products, ask for quotes on your home or renter's insurance with your auto. Just a side note: the higher your deductible the lower your premium. Make sure your limits of liability are adequate. As an example, Bodily Injury Liability $100,000 each person, $300,000 each accident, Property Damage Liability $100,000, Uninsured Motorists

Bodily Injury Liability $100,000 each person, $300,000 each accident, Medical Expense $5000. Get quotes from multiple carriers, using these amounts as a minimum. All companies offer these coverages however, most will offer you their minimum coverage limits. Get the maximum coverage even if it cost you a little more!

As an example, let's say your total annual life insurance expense is $432, homeowner's insurance $1,515 and auto insurance $1,982.40. To arrive at your monthly amounts, divide each expense by twelve. On your *Establishing New Spending Habits Worksheet*, you will enter:

Life:	$36.00
Homeowner's:	$126.25
Auto:	$165.20

Total: $327.45

Note: if homeowner's insurance is included in your mortgage payment do not include it on this worksheet. It is included in (Chapter 2, *Protecting Your Household)*.

Chapter 6

Managing Your Debts

The Spiritual Application: *Let no debt remain outstanding, except the continuing debt to love one another, for whoever loves others has fulfilled the law* (Romans 13:8). Psalms 37:21 says, *"Evil men borrow and "cannot pay it back!" But the good man returns what he owes with some extra besides."*

The Practical Application: We talked about expenses: shelter, food, utilities, transportation; however, the debt component is somewhat different.

Often when we look back through the process of hindsight, we discover not using delayed gratification but using other people's money (OPM), we end up in debt. If you are old enough you may remember when there were two methods for purchasing goods: cash or lay-away. Commerce and the internet have drastically changed the way we buy goods and services. Very few people write checks or use cash as was the custom only a few decades ago. In the absence of cash, it is much easier to spend your income, wealth and riches using plastic credit or debit cards. We buy now and pay later with our future income, wealth and riches. The wiser choice is to use the discipline of delayed gratification and your cash reserves and eliminate the debt process.

Our spiritual application sums up what our attitude should be about debt, let no debt remain outstanding. Even though you may have more debt than disposable income, you must somehow as the saying goes, "right the ship." Debt can be overwhelming, so how do we deal with it? Do we ignore it? Do we continue to live paycheck to paycheck? Can we re-position ourselves and become debt free?

The elimination of debt is not normally fast or pleasant. It takes a made-up mind and a determined spirit. First, capture all of your debt on your *Establishing New Spending Habits Worksheet*. Listing all of your debts will help you determine three things: how much debt you owe, the total minimum payment due each month and which debts are absolutely necessary and within your financial reach.

You have to decide with integrity which debt is absolutely necessary and within your financial budget, then commit to a repayment plan for those debts. I am not advocating irresponsibility!

Remember: once available income for the month is exhausted, you must call your creditors that did not receive money and explain your hardship. Let them know you have rearranged your budget and you are working through your shortage. You must commit to this process every month until this is no longer necessary. When you are over-encumbered you cannot pay everyone, use wisdom: first give your tithe and offering; pay your rent or mortgage; food; utilities; transportation and car loan if applicable then decide who will receive any remaining money!

The goal is to maintain your household and get completely out of debt. Your creditors will call demanding immediate payment of past-due bills. Be polite, let them know you have rearranged your budget and you are working through your shortage. At this stage do not spend money on anything else, this is when your integrity must kick-in.

Do not be ashamed of the process, believe me, this process builds integrity and good stewardship. Of course, your credit may suffer. Again, I am not advocating irresponsibility!

Once you get passed covering your basic needs, start the process of paying yourself a minimum of 10% of all you earn. Place this money in your emergency fund. Continue to pay each creditor as before but add yourself as if you were a creditor. Once you get to this stage some of your debt should be paid in full, now take the next debt on your *Establishing New Spending Habits Worksheet* and add it to your monthly budget. Even if this debt is now in collection or charged-off, begin the repayment process. You will do this until all debts are paid in full. Remember: Psalm 37:21 says… ***"But the good man returns what he owes with some extra besides."***

The *Establishing New Spending Habits Worksheet* aligns your income, wealth and riches to best meet your needs. The end result, you become a giver, a better provider, and a better steward. Once you get passed covering your basic needs you can begin the process of paying yourself and creating wealth.

It has been my experience by re-directing income, wealth and riches in this way, you build discipline and new behavior patterns. Even though the process seems slow proper handling of your income, wealth and riches will eventually retire your debts.

Back to our *Establishing New Spending Habits Worksheet*. As an example, let's say your monthly debts are car payment $460 per month, Lowe's $360, Altura $300 and student loans $440. Your monthly debts may be more or less.

On your *Establishing New Spending Habits Worksheet*, you will enter:

Car:	$460
Lowe's:	$360
Altura:	$300
Loans:	$440

Total: $1560

Just a side note: most Americans' monthly debts far exceed their monthly income. Be patient and work the process: "***Do not fret or have any anxiety about anything, but in every circumstance and in everything, by prayer and petition (definite requests), with thanksgiving,***

continue to make your wants known to God'
(Philippians 4:6).

Chapter 7

The Balance Sheet

The Spiritual Application: Matthew 25:16 says, *"**The man who received the $5,000 began immediately to buy and sell with it and soon earned another $5,000.**"*

The Practical Application: As a good steward your job is to eliminate debt and minimize expenses to create wealth. The Dictionary of Finance and Investment Terms defines net worth as the total value of all possessions, such as a house, stocks, bonds, and other securities, minus all outstanding debts, such as mortgage and revolving credit loans. The *Balance Sheet* will capture your assets and liabilities. Fill in all categories that apply, create a miscellaneous category to combine items valued less than $500.

Take your time, assess everything you possess, list the value on the worksheet. Use Kelley Blue Book to get a fair estimate of your vehicle's value. Have a real estate professional give you an estimate of your home's value. With all other items on your worksheet, be conservative with your estimate of value, research values for accuracy. Go online or to the market place to be realistic. For your liabilities use your most recent statements for amounts owed.

Back to our *Action Plan Balance Sheet.* As an example, let's say you have real estate, jewelry, car, furniture, stocks, bank accounts, life insurance, credit cards, and student loans. Your assets, liabilities, and net worth may be more or less. On your *Action Plan Balance Sheet*, you will enter:

Assets:
Residence:
Estimated value: $285,000

Jewelry:
Estimated value: $1,600

Furniture:
Estimated value: $6,500

Vehicle:
2015 Honda Accord EX-L
Estimated value: $14,211

Stocks:
Estimated value: $4,413

Bank Accounts:
Checking: $500
Savings: $1,500

Life Insurance:
Term Policy: $100,000
Total Assets: $413,724

Liabilities:
Personal Residence:
Amount owed: $29,000

Vehicle: 2015 Honda Accord EX-L
Amount owed: $11,450

Lowe's:
Amount owed: $4,300

Altura:
Amount owed: $3,600

Sallie Mae Student Loan:
Amount owed: $43,000
Total Liabilities: $91,350

Net Worth: $322,374

Just a side note: the largest assets are home equity and life insurance. Remember: According to Bestliferate.org, 2017 Life Insurance Statistics and Facts says, 41% of Americans do not carry any life insurance.

Chapter 8

The Income Profile

The Spiritual Application: **For even when we were with you, we gave you this rule: "The one who is unwilling to work shall not eat"** (2 Thessalonians 3:10).

The Practical Application: The *Income Profile Worksheet* gives you an estimation of your net income after deductions. As an example, using the median household income, $56,516 according to 2015 data from the U.S. Census, a single taxpayer with no dependents, deductions, or credits, using 2017 Federal and California income tax tables, net annual income would be $42,286.36.

To calculate: take your wages $56,516, minus your Federal tax withheld $7,270, Social Security tax withheld $3,504, Medicare tax withheld $819, State tax withheld $2,128 and SDI tax withheld $508.64, leaving you a net annual income of $42,286.36.

Step 2: divide $42,286.36 by 12. This will give you your net monthly income of $3,523.86. You can get these figures from your W-2 or by using your year to date amounts from your paycheck. These are basic deductions, check with your HR department if other amounts are being deducted from your wages or salary. This calculation helps you determine your net disposable income.

The *Income Profile Worksheet* is designed to estimate net income from multiple sources, see complete *Income Profile Worksheet* in *Action Plan* Forms. Note: your income, dependents, deductions, and credits may be different.

Chapter 9

Creating Wealth

The Spiritual Application: *"**Wealth and riches are in their houses, and their righteousness endures forever"** (*Psalm 112:3).

The Practical Application: The process of creating wealth can be as simple as getting out of debt, owning a share of stock in your favorite company, possessing the pink slip to your car, using a fifteen-year mortgage, being the CEO of your company, or having the reconveyance deed to your home. There is absolutely nothing like creating wealth, well let's say it another way, income, wealth and riches go hand and hand with ownership.

Go back and review (Chapter 7, *The Balance Sheet)*, how many assets do you own? How many of your assets are producing revenue?

We often miss the opportunity to gain or sustain ownership which creates wealth. For example, your car is paid in full and you decide to purchase a new vehicle. Unless you pay cash for the new vehicle you lose your ownership position and start the 36 to 60-month process to ownership over again. Another example, your home mortgage is close to being paid in full and instead of accelerating the debt repayment process, you decide to purchase a newer, larger home and restart the ownership process.

You have to be deliberate about creating wealth! *"**Be not deceived; God is not mocked: for whatsoever a man soweth, that shall he also reap**"* (Galatians 6:7). You must sow into wealth to reap wealth, otherwise, it's a contradiction to biblical principles. Remember: as a good steward your job is to eliminate debt and minimize expenses to create wealth. Your paycheck, commissions, retirement income, is your greatest tool in the creating wealth process. Always reinvest a portion of your income to create more wealth. This process is vital!

Start the process of ownership today. Buy and accumulate assets. Some sound assets are cash, precious metals, stocks, bonds, real estate, and business ownership. Invest in things that will appreciate in value over time. Remember the Dictionary of Finance and Investment Terms defines net worth, or you could say wealth, as the total value of all possessions, such as a house, stocks, bonds, and other securities, minus all outstanding debts, such as mortgage and revolving credit loans.

God has given us the power to get wealth. If you are not sure where to start; here are two scriptures to meditate on: James 1:5 *"If any of you lacks wisdom, he should ask God, who gives generously to all without finding fault, and it will be given to him."* And Proverbs 13:11 *"Dishonest money dwindles away, but whoever gathers money little by little makes it grow."*

God will give you many opportunities to attain income, wealth and riches in your lifetime. Be sensitive to His leading and obey His commands. Start where you are, be patient and enjoy the journey! Galatians 6:9 says, *"Let us not become weary in doing good, for at the proper time we will reap a harvest if we do not give up."*

Chapter 10

Wealth Distribution

The Spiritual Application: "*A good person leaves an inheritance for their children's children...*" (Proverbs 13:22).

The Practical Application: Now that you have attained income, wealth and riches, how do you distribute your assets? The spiritual application says it best, you should leave wealth to the next generation, your children, grandchildren, and charities. I am not giving legal advice! However, you can do some simple things like transfer real property by deed or living trust. Make sure your beneficiaries on life insurance policies and pensions are in order. Have a will for your personal belongings. Seek the advice of an attorney!

Take the time to think of the person or persons who could best continue your family legacy, this will take prayer and discernment. Often at the death of a loved one, the normal process is, sell all assets and divide the income (wealth) among the heirs. Each heir receives their inheritance and goes their separate way. What was once an asset, becomes liquidated into cash and that cash soon finds its way back into the market place leaving the heirs without the asset or the cash.

Devise a plan that will keep the asset in the family for perpetual generations. If the asset is real estate, disperse the cashflow as dividends keeping the asset intact. Even though rents divided by many heirs may seem insufficient, build family assets until you amass enough wealth that the entire family is wealthy off of the cashflow. This is how the rich get richer. Seek the legal advice of an estate attorney! Most families just liquidate assets and move on with their lives.

Summary

Managing your finances properly is a key component to living an abundant life. Many people feel budgeting is time-consuming and hard work. I hope this book has simplified the process and given you new insight. Think of each action step as a piece of the puzzle that completes your financial picture. Every journey begins with taking the first few steps.

Your new spending and saving habits will allow you to move closer to your goals each time you receive income. Your *Action Plan* is organized, time-driven and measurable. In the natural, the *Action Plan* is an annual budget designed to take you from where you currently are to where you want to be in the near future.

However, applying the scriptures along with the *Action Plan* is like *"The Parable of the Growing Seed."* Mark 4:26-29 states, *"This is what the kingdom of God is like. A man scatters seed on the ground. Night and Day, whether he sleeps or gets up, the seed sprouts and grows, though he does not know how. All by itself the soil produces, grain, fruit, the stalk, then the head, then the full kernel in the head. As soon as the grain is ripe, he puts the sickle to it, because the harvest has come."*

You don't have to know how you are going to get out of debt, save for retirement, or build your emergency fund. Leave the how-to for God. Use your *Action Plan*, and the scriptures provided. Even though there are many steps on your *Action Plan*. There are really only three actions you must take to succeed: Decide to do it, do it, and keep doing it. James 1:4 says, *"Let perseverance finish its work so that you may be mature and complete, not lacking anything."*

One Last Action

"For God so loved the world that he gave his one and only Son, that whosoever believes in him shall not perish but have eternal life" (John 3:16). If you don't know Jesus Christ, as your Lord and Savior. Pray this simple prayer: Lord Jesus, come into my life, forgive me of my sins, take my life and do something with it. I submit all to you. Amen. Now all scripture references in this book applies to you.

Scripture References

The blessing of the Lord, brings wealth, without painful toil for it. (**Proverbs 10:22**) New International Version.

But remember the Lord your God, for it is he who gives you the ability to produce wealth. (**Deuteronomy 8:18**) New International Version.

There is a way that appears to be right, but in the end, it leads to death. (**Proverbs 14:12**) New International Version.

What good will it be for a man if he gains the whole world, yet forfeits his soul? Or what can a man give in exchange for his soul?" (**Matthew 16:26**) New International Version.

For we brought nothing into this world, and it is certain we can carry nothing out." (**1 Timothy 6:7**) King James Version.

To one he gave five talents of money, to another two talents, and to another one talent each according to his ability. Then he went on his journey. The man who received the five talents went at once and put his money to work and gained five more. So, also the one with two talents gained two more. But the man who had received the one talent went off, dug a hole in the ground and hid his master's money. After a long time, the master of those servants returned and settled accounts with them. The man who had received the five talents brought the other five. Master, he said, "you entrusted me with five talents. See, I have gained five more." "His master replied, Well done, good and faithful servant! You have been faithful with a few things; I will put you in charge of many things, Come and share your master's happiness!" **(Matthew 25:15-21)** New International Version.

But my God shall supply all your need according to his riches in glory by Christ Jesus. **(Philippians 4:19)** King James Version.

The Lord is my shepherd; I shall not want. **(Psalm 23:1)** King James Version.

Delight yourself in the Lord and he will give you the desires of your heart." **(Psalm 37:4)** New International Version.

Now, this is what the Lord Almighty says: "Give careful thought to your ways. You have planted much but have harvested little. You eat, but never have enough. You drink, but never have your fill. You put on clothes but are not warm. You earn wages, only to put them in a purse with holes in it." This is what the Lord Almighty says: "Give careful thought to your ways." **(Haggai 1:5-7)** New International Version.

God is not a man, that he should lie, nor a son of man, that he should change his mind. Does he speak and then not act? Does he promise and not fulfill? **(Numbers 23:19)** New International Version.

Bring the whole tithe into the storehouse, that there may be food in my house. Test me in this, "says the Lord Almighty, and see if I will not throw open the floodgates of heaven and pour out so much blessing that you will not have room enough for it." **(Malachi 3:10)** New International Version.

Honor the Lord by giving him the first part of all your income, and he will fill your barns with wheat and barley and overflow your wine vats with the finest wines. **(Proverbs 3:9)** The Living Bible.

Remember this: Whoever sows sparingly will also reap sparingly, and whoever sows generously will also reap generously. Each man should give what he has decided in his heart to give, not reluctantly or under compulsion, for God loves a cheerful giver. And God is able to make all grace abound to you, so that in all things at all times, having all that you need, you will abound in every good work. **(2 Corinthians 9:6-8)** New International Version.

My people are destroyed from a lack of knowledge. **(Hosea 4:6)** New International Version.

He will rebuke the devourer for your sake. **(Malachi 3:11)** King James Version.

For as the body without the spirit is dead, so faith without works is dead also. **(James 2:26)** King James Version.

Whoever can be trusted with very little can also be trusted with much, and whoever is dishonest with very little will also be dishonest with much. So, if you have not been trustworthy in handling worldly wealth, who will trust you with true riches? And if you have not been trustworthy with someone else's property, who will give you property of your own? **(Luke 16:10-12)** New International Version.

And the Lord answered me, and said, Write the vision, and make it plain upon tables, that he may run that readeth it. For the vision is yet for an appointed time, but at the end it shall speak, and not lie: though it may tarry, wait for it; because it will surely come... **(Habakkuk 2:2-3)** King James Version.

But if any provide not for his own, and specially, for those of his own house, he hath denied the faith, and is worse than an infidel. **(1Timothy 5:8)** King James Version.

Is anything too hard for the Lord? **(Genesis 18:14)** King James Version.

Evil men borrow and "cannot pay it back"! But the good man returns what he owes with some extra besides. **(Psalm 37:21)** The Living Bible.

But seek first his kingdom and his righteousness, and all these things will be given to you as well. **(Matthew 6:33)** New International Version

Dishonest money dwindles away, but whoever gathers money little by little makes it grow. **(Proverbs 13:11)** New International Version.

No discipline seems pleasant at the time, but painful. Later on, however, it produces a harvest of righteousness and peace for those who have been trained by it. **(Hebrew 12:11)** New International Version.

Now faith is the substance of things hoped for, the evidence of things not seen. **(Hebrews 11:1)** King James Version.

For the Lord your God is bringing you into a good land; a land with streams and pools of water, with springs flowing in the valleys and hills; a land with wheat and barley, vine and fig trees, pomegranates, olive oil and honey; a land where bread will not be scarce and you will lack nothing... **(Deuteronomy 8:7-9)** New International Version.

For I know the plans I have for you, declares the Lord, plans to prosper you and not to harm you, plans to give you hope and a future. **(Jeremiah 29:11)** New International Version.

He will bless them that fear the Lord, both small and great. The Lord shall increase you more and more, you and your children. **(Psalm 115:13-14)** King James Version.

Wisdom is the principal thing; therefore, get wisdom: and with all thy getting get understanding. **(Proverbs 4:7)** King James Version.

Let no debt remain outstanding, except the continuing debt to love one another, for whoever loves others has fulfilled the law. **(Romans 13:8)** New International Version.

Do not fret or have any anxiety about anything, but in every circumstance and in everything, by prayer and petition (definite requests), with thanksgiving, continue to make your wants known to God. **(Philippians 4:6)** Amplified Version.

Let us not become weary in doing good, for at the proper time we will reap a harvest if we do not give up. **(Galatians 6:9)** New International Version.

The man who received the $5,000 began immediately to buy and sell with it and soon earned another $5,000. **(Matthew 25:16)** The Living Bible.

For even when we were with you, we gave you this rule: The one who is unwilling to work shall not eat. **(2 Thessalonians 3:10)** New International Version.

Wealth and riches are in their houses, and their righteousness endures forever. **(Psalm 112:3)** New International Version.

Be not deceived; God is not mocked: for whatsoever a man soweth, that shall he also reap. **(Galatians 6:7)** King James Version.

If any of you lacks wisdom, he should ask God, who gives generously to all without finding fault, and it will be given to him. **(James 1:5)** New International Version.

A good person leaves an inheritance for their children's children... **(Proverbs 13:22)** New International Version.

The Parable of the Growing Seed, He also said, this, is what the kingdom of God is like. A man scatters seed on the ground. Night and Day, whether he sleeps or gets up, the seed sprouts and grows, though he does not know how. All by itself the soil produces, grain, fruit, the stalk, then the head, then the full kernel in the head. As soon as the grain is ripe, he puts the sickle to it, because the harvest has come. **(Mark 4:26-29)** New International Version.

Let perseverance finish its work so that you may be mature and complete, not lacking anything. **(James 1:4)** New International Version.

For God so loved the world that he gave his one and only Son, that whosoever believes in him shall not perish but have eternal life. **(John 3:16)** New International Version.

Appendix

New Spending Habits Worksheet
Protecting Your Household

Giving:
Tithes: $352.39
Offerings: $88.10
Total: $440.49

Shelter:
Mortgage: $1785

Food:
Groceries: $660

Utilities:
Electric: $175
Heating: $50
Water: $100
Cable: $106
Cell phone: $50
Total: $481

Transportation:
Gasoline: $320

Emergency Fund:
Savings: $1,360.50

Retirement:
Pension Plan: $704.77

Insurance Products:
Life: $36
Homeowner's: $126.50
Auto: $165.20
Total: $327.70

Debts:
Car payment: $460
Lowe's: $360
Altura: $300
Student Loan: $440
Total: $1,560

Total monthly expense: $7,639.46

I know most Americans do not budget nor track their spending and saving habits. If they did, however, most American budgets would look close to our example. The average American household's disposable income is far less than their expenses and debts, and most do not have savings for emergencies nor retirement.

The *New Spending Habit Worksheet* is designed to re-allocate income to best meet your immediate needs. Each chapter is designed to illustrate how to best deal with each subject matter   God's   way.

Now let's examine the *New Spending Habit Worksheet*. The first five categories exceed monthly income by $162.63 per month. At this point, you may believe the logical thing to do is take the tithe and offering out of the budget and use the additional $440.49 to pay household expenses. However, when you take God out of the equation you begin trusting in your ability and you give up the spiritual promise of financial protection as stated in (Malachi 3:10). Even if we did use the tithe and offering to offset household expenses our total disposable income of $3523.86 is well short of current expenses and debt obligations.

The million-dollar question is what do you do when you run out of money? We must have a paradigm shift in our thinking, the Bible calls this process faith. When you are over-encumbered you cannot pay everyone, use wisdom: first, give your tithe and offering; pay your rent or mortgage; food; utilities; transportation and car loan if applicable, then decide who will receive any remaining money! At this point, all other categories are outside of our financial budget and must be deferred to a later date.

Whatever your shortage, here is where you must decide whether you will continue to live this way. You have to decide with integrity which expenses and debts are within your financial budget then commit to a repayment plan for those expenses and debts. Go back and review (Chapter 6 *Managing Your Debts)*.

When your creditors call demanding immediate payment of past-due bills. Be polite, explain your hardship, let them know you have rearranged your budget and you are working through your shortage. At this stage, do not spend money on anything else, this is when your integrity must kick-in. Do not be ashamed of the process, believe me, this process builds integrity and good stewardship. Of course, your credit may suffer.

This debt scenario is common in most American household's disposable income is far short of expenses and debts. You must re-allocate your disposable income to position yourself for financial freedom. Once you get passed covering your basic needs, start the process of paying yourself a minimum of 10% of all you earn. Place this money in your emergency fund. Continue to pay each creditor as before but add yourself as if you were a creditor.

Once you get to this stage some of your debt should be paid in full, now take the next debt on your *Establishing New Spending Habits Worksheet*, and add it to your monthly budget. Even if this debt is now in collection or charged-off, begin the repayment process. You will do this until all debts are paid in full.

Action Plan
Forms

New Spending Habits
Protecting Your Household

Giving:

Tithes: _____

Offerings: _____

Total: $ _____   Open a bank account

Shelter:

Rent: _____

Mortgage: _____

HOA: _____

Total: $ _____   Open a bank account

Food:

Groceries: _____

Household: _____

Eating out: _____

Total: $ _____   Open a bank account

New Spending Habits
Protecting Your Household

Utilities:

Cell: _____

Electric: _____

Heating: _____

Water: _____

Cable: _____

Land line: _____

Internet/DSL: _____

Total: $_____   Open a bank account

Transportation:

Gas: _____

Repairs: _____

Total: $_____   Open a bank account

New Spending Habits
Additional Expenses

Birthday & Special Occasions:

Total: $_____   Open a bank account

Child Care:

Total: $_____   Open a bank account

Child Support:

Total: $_____   Open a bank account

Clothes:

Total: $_____   Open a bank account

Drinks:

Total: $_____   Open a bank account

Education Expense:

Tuition: _____

Books: _____

Total: $_____   Open a bank account

New Spending Habits
Additional Expenses

Gambling:

Total: $_____   Open a bank account

Grooming:

Hair care: _____

Nails: _____

Total: $_____   Open a bank account

Holidays:

Total: $_____   Open a bank account

Household:

Repairs: _____

Gardner: _____

Total: $_____   Open a bank account

New Spending Habits
Additional Expenses

Pets:

Total: $_____   Open a bank account

Smoke:

Total: $_____   Open a bank account

Vacations:

Total: $_____   Open a bank account

New Spending Habits
Future Resources Savings

Emergency fund:

Total: $_____   Open a bank account

Retirement:

Total: $_____   Open a bank account

New Spending Habits
Protecting Your Assets

Insurance:

Auto: _____

Total: $_____   Open a bank account

Dental: _____

Health: _____

Total: $_____   Open a bank account

Home: _____

Total: $_____   Open a bank account

Life: _____

Total: $_____   Open a bank account

Renter's: _____

Total: $_____   Open a bank account

New Spending Habits
Managing Your Debts

Loans:

Car payment: $_____   Balance: $ _____

Personal loan: $_____   Balance: $ _____

Student loan: $_____   Balance: $ _____

Lease payment: $_____   Balance: $ _____

Lease payment: $_____   Balance: $ _____

Other payment: $_____   Balance: $ _____

Other payment: $_____   Balance: $ _____

Other payment: $_____   Balance: $ _____

Total: $_____ $ _____

Credit Cards: Minimum Payment: Balance:

_____ $_____ $_____

_____ $_____ $_____

_____ $_____ $_____

The Balance Sheet
Assets

Real Property
Address   Present Value

_____ $_____

_____ $_____

_____ $_____

Total $_____

Personal Property
(Vehicles)   Present Value

_____ $_____

_____ $_____

_____ $_____

Total $_____

The Balance Sheet
Assets

Personal Property
(Jewelry, Furniture)   Present Value

_____ $_____

_____ $_____

_____ $_____

_____ $_____

Total $_____

Stocks/ Bonds/ Mutual Funds:
Name   Present Value

_____ $_____

_____ $_____

_____ $_____

Total $_____

The Balance Sheet
Assets

Bank Accounts:
Name   Balance

_____ $_____

_____ $_____

_____ $_____

Total $_____

Retirement Accounts:
Name   Present Value

_____ $_____

_____ $_____

Total $_____

The Balance Sheet
Assets

Insurance Policies:
Company   Present Value

_____ $_____

_____ $_____

Total $_____

Miscellaneous:

_____ $_____

_____ $_____

Total $_____

Total Assets $_____

The Balance Sheet
Liabilities

Real Property:
Address   Amount Owed

_____ $_____

_____ $_____

Total $_____

Personal Property:
(Vehicles)   Amount Owed

_____ $_____

_____ $_____

Total $_____

Personal Property:
(Jewelry, Furniture)   Amount Owed

_____ $_____

_____ $_____

_____ $_____

Total $_____

The Balance Sheet
Liabilities

Student Loans:
Name   Amount Owed

_____ $_____

_____ $_____

_____ $_____

Total $_____

Credit Cards:
Name   Amount Owed

_____ $_____

_____ $_____

_____ $_____

_____ $_____

Total $_____

Total Liabilities: $_____

Net Worth: $_____

Income Profile
Worksheet

Husband's YTD:

Wages $_____
Use W-2 or year to date
amounts from your pay check.

*Federal Tax Withheld $_____

*Social Security Tax Withheld $_____

*Medicare Tax Withheld $_____

*SDI Tax Withheld $_____

*State Tax Withheld $_____

*Retirement accounts 401K etc. $_____

*Union Dues $_____

*Medical deductions $_____

*Others $_____
**Note: Subtract all amounts
with an asterisk from wages**.

Total deductions $_____

Net annual Wages $_____

Income Profile
Worksheet

Husband's YTD:
Pension $_____
Use 1099-R

**Note: Subtract all amounts
with an asterisk from Pension.**

*Federal Tax Withheld $_____

*State Tax Withheld $_____

Net annual Pension $_____

Income Profile
Worksheet

Wife's YTD:

Wages $_____
Use W-2 or year to date
amounts from your pay check.

*Federal Tax Withheld $_____

*Social Security Tax Withheld $_____

*Medicare Tax Withheld $_____

*SDI Tax Withheld $_____

*State Tax Withheld $_____

*Retirement accounts 401K etc. $_____

*Union Dues $_____

*Medical deductions $_____

*Others $_____

**Note: Subtract all amounts
with an asterisk from wages.**

Total deductions $_____

Net annual Wages $_____

Income Profile

Worksheet

Wife's YTD:
Pension $_____
Use 1099-R

**Note: Subtract all amounts
with an asterisk from Pension.**

*Federal Tax Withheld $_____

*State Tax Withheld $_____

Net annual Pension $_____

God wants you to prosper. He has declared in His word, ***For I know the plans I have for you, declares the Lord, plans to prosper you and not to harm you, plans to give you hope and a future*** (Jeremiah 29:11).

Made in the USA
San Bernardino, CA
26 February 2020